Frank Cullotta's
Greatest (Kitchen) Hits

A
GANGSTER'S
COOKBOOK

By FRANK CULLOTTA
and DENNIS N. GRIFFIN

WILDBLUE
PRESS

WildBluePress.com

FRANK CULLOTTA'S GREATEST (KITCHEN) HITS published by:
WILDBLUE PRESS
P.O. Box 102440
Denver, Colorado 80250

ISBN 978-1-952225-40-6 Trade Paperback
ISBN 978-1-952225-39-0 eBook

Cover design © 2020 WildBlue Press. All rights reserved.

Cover design by Villa Design

Interior Formatting by Elijah Toten
www.totencreative.com

Frank Cullotta's Greatest (Kitchen) Hits

TABLE OF CONTENTS

ACKNOWLEDGEMENTS

Listen close. I want to thank my sister-in-law, Pamela Cullotta, and my many friends for their support and for contributing their favorite recipes for use in this book. A special thanks to Faith and Denny Griffin for their help in putting it all together, and to their daughter, Pam Ashley, for proofreading and editing. And to Adam Flowers and Alicia Morse for assembling the photos and doing research. Without their help and support, this book would not have happened.

Frank Cullotta

INTRODUCTION

I am probably best known for my exploits as an associate of the Chicago Outfit and my role as Tony Spilotro's street lieutenant in Las Vegas; however, I have many other interests. Among them is my love of cooking.

In *Frank Cullotta's Greatest (Kitchen) Hits*, I have assembled some of my personal favorite recipes, as well as a collection of mouth-watering dishes recommended by family—including my mother Josephine (Mama Josie)—and friends. Some of the recipes have been kicking around for decades and were modified by the chef. Others are entirely new. So, pick out the ones that stimulate your taste buds and give them a try. And if you happen to put on a pound or two in the process, *forget about it!*

Frank Cullotta

ITALIAN

When I first moved to Las Vegas in 1979, Leo Gardino and I pulled a couple of burglary jobs. We robbed a total of $68,000 from two houses and decided to put our money together and open a pizza joint called The Upper Crust. This is the recipe for our main dish.

Upper Crust Pizza and Pizza Dough

This pizza was the specialty at Frank Cullotta's Upper Crust Restaurant in Las Vegas.

Instructions

Prepare pizza dough (see recipe)

Oil a deep-dish pan (2 – 2 ½ inches)

Line the bottom and sides of the pan with the dough and overlap slightly at the top.

In a separate frying pan, pre-cook any meats or sausage to be used until about ¾ done. Remove and place on a towel to absorb any extra grease, then add to the deep-dish pan. Add any other optional ingredients, such as pepperoni, onions, peppers, or black olives.

Add sauce and Provolone cheese. Cook for 40 – 45 minutes (check periodically).

Remove from oven and cover the top with the remaining dough. Slit the top crust in three or four places to allow equal heating.

Cover with sauce and Parmesan cheese and cook for an additional 15 minutes.

Stuffed Pizza

Pizza Dough

This is the way we made our dough back at the Upper Crust in Las Vegas. When I was in prison and later in witness protection, I had a lot of time on my hands and I enjoyed reading. I learned about the legend of pizza, and supposedly, the first person to make modern pizza was a baker in Naples named Raffaele Esposito. He would make his patriotic pie topped with mozzarella, basil, and tomatoes. Those ingredients were the colors of the Italian flag.

Ingredients

1 pkg dry active yeast
1 ½ cup of lukewarm water
4 cups flour
1 tsp salt & ¼ tsp sugar mixed
¼ cup extra virgin olive oil

Instructions

Dissolve yeast in lukewarm water, add salt/sugar mixture

Add flour and mix

On a flour-powdered wooden surface, pour out the dough and knead until smooth and elastic (about 5 minutes).

Put dough in a large olive oil-greased bowl and rub a little oil over the dough and cover with a cloth.

Let it rise in warm place until at least double in size of bowl.

Divide the dough into 2 or 3 equal round balls.

Use rolling pin to roll out pizza dough into 14-16-inch rounds.

Place pizza on round baking tins.

Makes 3 14 to16-inch pizzas

When I was growing up in Chicago, I always looked out for my kid brother, Joe. I visited him and his wife on my last trip to Chicago, and she made this dish for me. Mama Mia! Now Joe is looking out for me.

Braciole With Steak

Ingredients

1 ½ lb. flank steak
1 tsp extra virgin olive oil
1 sliced hardboiled egg
2 tbsp Romano or Parmesan cheese, grated
½ tsp basil
1 tbsp Italian breadcrumbs
1 tbsp pine nuts
¼ tsp black pepper
½ tsp parsley
½ tsp oregano
½ tsp onion powder
2 cloves garlic, chopped.
1 piece of string to tie around steak

Instructions

Place flank steak on board and tenderize with a meat pounder.

Rub some extra virgin olive oil over both sides of the steak.

Arrange egg slices on top of steak.

Mix the remaining ingredients in a bowl and spread on top of steak.

Roll the steak and tie with string to hold it together.

Heat olive oil in large skillet and cook the Braciole until light brown.

Top with red pasta sauce.

Serves 4 – 6

Suggested red wine: Frescobaldi, "Luce" Toscano

Beef Braciole

Braciole

This is so good it will make you cry. You're going to have to invest some time and effort into this recipe, but it is well worth it!

Braciole

Ingredients

4 tbsp olive oil
¼ tsp salt
¼ tsp pepper
¼ tsp garlic powder
1/3 cup Romano cheese, grated.
2 tbsp parsley, chopped.
1 cup breadcrumbs
10 slices eye-of-round beef, pounded thin
Marinara sauce
4 tbsp olive oil for frying beef

Instructions

Mix first seven ingredients in bowl.

Lay beef on flat surface, sprinkle the bread crumb mixture on top of sliced beef.

Roll up the steak and secure with kitchen twine.

In a large frying pan, add 4 tbsp olive oil and brown braciola on both sides.

Put in ovenproof baking dish and top with marinara sauce

Cover with foil and bake at 350 degrees for 40 minutes or until tender

The last time I made these was during the great Corona quarantine of 2020. You won't be disappointed.

Cavatelli

Ingredients

4 cups flour
5-6 eggs
½ tsp salt
1 small potato, mashed

Instructions

Make a well in the center of the flour, add salt.

Add eggs in center hole and beat lightly. Add mashed potato.

Mix to make soft dough. Keep turning the dough on floured surface and knead for about five minutes.

Break off pieces of dough and roll into rolls about the thickness of a fat pencil. Cut into pieces 3/4 inches long.

With your first and second fingers, make a dent in each piece and roll along a floured table, fork toward you.

Bring 3 quarts of water to boil, add 1 tbsp salt to water. Cook cavatelli for about 30 minutes. Test for firmness. Drain and serve with pasta sauce and sprinkle with Romano cheese.

Serves 4-6 Suggested red wine: Ruffino, Reserve Ducale Chianti Classico

Cavatelli

When I was a kid in Chicago, I often got into fights with other kids, including Tony Spilotro. I'd come home and my mother would bandage my hands and any other scuffs or cuts. Then she would make me my favorite—her Italian grilled cheese sandwich.

Italian Grilled Cheese Sandwich

Ingredients

½ cup oil-packed sun-dried tomatoes
¼ cup parmesan cheese, grated
2 tbsp olive oil
1 tbs. balsamic vinegar
1 tsp garlic powder
1/8 tsp each salt & pepper
8 slices Italian bread
1 1/4 cup mozzarella cheese, shredded
¼ cup fresh arugula
2 tbsp roasted sweet red pepper, chopped
3 tbsp butter, melted

Instructions

Mix first six ingredients together.

Spread over four of the bread slices.

Top with cheeses, arugula, red pepper, and remaining bread. Brush outsides of sandwiches with butter.

On griddle, toast sandwiches over medium heat until golden brown and

Cheese is melted, 3-4 minutes per side.

The word cacciatore means "hunter" in Italian. So, this dish is for you chicken hunters.

Chicken Cacciatore

Ingredients

21/2 – 3 lbs. chicken breasts cut up, with skin left on
1 tbsp extra virgin olive oil
1 clove garlic, chopped
1-8oz. can crushed tomatoes
1-8oz. can tomato sauce
¼ tsp rosemary leaves
½ tsp oregano
½ tsp onion salt
¼ tsp black pepper
2 tbsp lemon juice and some lemon rind
2 tbsp red table wine
1 tbsp balsamic vinegar
10 small green or black olives, sliced
More olives can be added if you like.

Instructions

In a large, deep skillet, brown the pieces of chicken in olive oil. Then add chopped garlic and cook for two more minutes.

Add all the other ingredients and stir.

Cover and cook on low for about 30-40 minutes or until the chicken is tender

Stir and turn chicken while cooking.

Can be served alone or with any type of pasta.

Serves 4-6 Suggested red wine: Pio Cesare Dolcetto d'Alba

If you don't like meat, this is for you.

Eggplant Parmesan Bake

Ingredients

2 large eggplants
2 eggs
¼ cup butter, melted
1 cup breadcrumbs (or panko)
Salt & pepper to taste
¾ cup parmesan cheese, finely grated
1 48oz jar tomato sauce
1 lb. mozzarella, shredded

Instructions

Preheat oven to 400 degrees and prepare baking sheet with wire rack.

Prepare eggplant by slicing into 1/4 -inch thick slices.

Whisk eggs together with cool melted butter and season with salt & pepper.

Prepare breadcrumbs, mix with salt & pepper, and 2 tbsp Parmesan cheese.

Bread eggplant starting with egg & butter mixture, followed by breadcrumbs.

Place on prepared baking sheet and repeat with remaining eggplant slices.

Bake for 20 – 25 minutes or until golden and crispy.

Eggplant Parmesan Bake

Fettucine Alfredo

This dish dates back to the early 1900s in Italy and is one of my all-time favorite dinners. It is very rich and filling. If you eat too much of it, you might get a little thick in the hips. So, be careful.

Fettucine Alfredo

Ingredients

4 tbsp butter
1 ½ cups heavy cream
1 tbsp salt
1-lb fettucine
2 egg yolks
1 cup Parmigiano-Reggiano cheese, freshly grated
½ tsp black pepper

Instructions

In a large saucepan, add butter and cream, turn the heat to medium and cook until cream and butter are melted together, around 1 minute. Turn off heat.

Bring a large pot of water to a boil. Add 1 tbsp salt and the fettuccini. Cook per instructions on package.

Drain pasta in colander and add to pan with butter and cream. Turn the heat to medium.

Add the egg yolks, Parmigiano-Reggiano cheese, and black pepper. Stir vigorously, mixing the egg yolks and cheese in and coating all the pasta with the sauce.

Serve immediately from the pan, sprinkle additional amounts of Parmigiano-Riggiano cheese on top.

Serves 4-6

Suggested white wine: Trentino, Pinot Grigio

You can do a few things with these little guys. You can put them with noodles and call it spaghetti and meatballs. You can put them in between bread and have a meatball sandwich, or you can just eat the meatballs by themselves. I like them all three ways.

Meatballs

Ingredients

1 lb. ground beef
½ lb. ground pork
½ lb. ground veal
2 eggs
¼ cup Romano cheese
1-2 slices soft white bread, wet and squeezed
½ cup Italian breadcrumbs
3 cloves garlic, chopped fine
¼ tsp salt
½ tsp pepper
½ tsp onion powder
¼ tsp oregano
½ tsp basil
½ tsp parsley
Extra virgin oil (to fry meatballs in)

Instructions

In a large bowl, mix eggs and meat together. Add the rest of the ingredients and knead with your hands until well mixed.

Roll in your hands to form meat balls (*if meat is too wet to roll, add more cheese*).

In a deep skillet, fry the meatballs in the olive oil until golden brown.

Turn frequently to avoid burning.

Meatballs

This was a staple when I was growing up. It seemed like my mom made this at least once a week. When I make this myself, the smell and taste take me back to when I was still an innocent kid.

Mostaccioli

Ingredients

1lb mostaccioli pasta
1lb Italian sweet or hot sausage (remove casing)
1 tbsp virgin olive oil
2 red bell peppers
1 medium onion, sliced
2 tbsp garlic, minced
4 cups pasta sauce
½ tsp salt and ground pepper

Instructions

Bring a large pot of water to boil. Cook pasta as pasta package suggests.

In a large nonstick skillet, cook sausage over medium heat 5 minutes or until browned. Break up the sausage in chunks. Remove to a plate.

Add oil, peppers, onion, and garlic to skillet.

Cook, stirring occasionally, 5 minutes or until lightly browned.

Add sausage, sauce, salt, and pepper, stir occasionally to prevent burning.

Drain pasta, do not rinse. Transfer to a large bowl and add the contents of the skillet. Mix and serve.

Serves 6 Suggested wine: Valpolicella, Caterina or Doctora Zardozi

People always ask if I have any secrets that I'll take to my grave. Well, I did, until now. This is my family's secret recipe for pasta sauce. Make this and you will taste what real pasta sauce tastes like.

Pasta Sauce

Ingredients

1½ lbs. boneless pork shoulder ribs, cut in cubes
1 tbsp extra virgin olive oil
1 large can of crushed tomatoes
1 small can tomato sauce
1 small can tomato paste
¼ tsp basil
¼ tsp oregano
½ tsp parsley
2 cloves garlic, chopped
¼ tsp onion powder
¼ tsp garlic salt
Romano cheese, freshly grated

Instructions

In a deep saucepan, fry the pork rib cubes in olive oil until golden brown. Then add the chopped garlic. Cook a few minutes more, then add crushed tomatoes, tomato sauce, tomato paste and spices.

Sprinkle some Romano cheese into the sauce and simmer on low heat for 11/2 to

2 hours. Stir every ten minutes. Salt and pepper to taste. If desired, a shot of red table wine may be added to the sauce.

Note: *When you no longer see orange foam from the tomatoes, the sauce is done.*

A real palate-pleaser that you'll make more than once. Mouth-watering!

Ravioli

Dough Ingredients

4 cups flour
5 or 6 eggs
½ tsp salt
2 tbsp water, as needed.

Instructions

Pile up the flour on a flat surface. Make a well in center of the flour. Add one egg at a time. Add the salt as you mix lightly. Turn dough on floured surface. Knead about 5 minutes

Ravioli

Cheese Ravioli Filling

Filling Ingredients

16 oz Ricotta cheese
2 eggs
1 ½ cup dry Romano cheese
½ tsp salt
½ tsp pepper

Instructions

Mix filling ingredients well.

Divide dough into 4 equal sections.

Lightly roll each portion 1/8 inch-thick in a rectangle.

Cut 4-inch squares. Place 2 tsp filling on each square.

Fold over and seal, press together with tines of fork dipped in flour.

Cook in boiling water 20 - 25 minutes. Serve with pasta sauce.

Serves 4-6 Suggested red wine: Ecco Domani, Merlot

If you are lactose intolerant, take a pass. If you love cheese...
here you are.

Five-Cheese Ziti Bake

Ingredients

1 ½ lbs (about 7 cups) ziti or small tube pasta
2 jars (24 oz.each) marinara sauce
1 jar (15 oz.) Alfredo sauce
2 cups shredded part-skim mozzarella cheese, divided
½ cup reduced-fat ricotta cheese
½ cup provolone cheese, shredded
½ cup Romano cheese, grated

Topping Ingredients.

½ cup parmesan cheese
½ cup panko (Japanese) breadcrumbs
3 garlic cloves, minced
2 tbsp olive oil

Instructions

Preheat oven to 350 degrees. Cook pasta according to package instructions for al dente; drain.

In large saucepan, combine marinara sauce, Alfredo sauce, 1 cup mozzarella, ricotta, provolone, and Romano cheeses. Heat over medium heat until sauce begins to simmer and cheeses are melted. Stir in cooked pasta, pour mixture into greased 13x9-inch baking dish. Top with remaining 1 cup mozzarella cheese.

In a small bowl, stir together the parmesan breadcrumbs, garlic, and olive oil.

Sprinkle over pasta.

Bake uncovered until mixture is bubbly and topping is golden brown, 30-40 minutes.

Grandma's Baked Ziti

This is a dish that I love. The cutlets are not only breaded and fried, but also baked to perfection while marinating in tomato sauce and cheese.

Veal Parmesan

Ingredients

1 ½ to 2 lbs veal steak
1 brown bag
1 ½ cup dry breadcrumbs
½ cup Romano cheese, grated
3 eggs, beaten
¾ tsp garlic salt
¼ tsp black pepper
1/3 cup extra virgin olive oil
6 slices mozzarella cheese

Instructions

Place the veal medallions between sheets of waxed paper and pound with a mallet or the flat side of a cleaver until they are ½ inch thick.

In the bag, combine ingredients, breadcrumbs, and Romano cheese.

Add the veal and shake until covered. Set aside.

Heat skillet, add 1/3 cup extra virgin oil, add veal, and brown on all sides.

Next, arrange the veal in a 7 X 11-inch baking dish.

Use the pasta sauce recipe in this book and pour over the veal.

Put one slice of mozzarella cheese over each cutlet and bake at 350 degrees for 20 minutes or until cheese is melted.

Veal Parmesan

Meatball Parmesan Bake

Ingredients

¾ lb. ground pork
¾ lb. ground beef
4 cloves garlic, minced
1 cup Italian breadcrumbs
½ cup water
½ cup parmesan cheese, shredded
2 eggs
salt and pepper
1 large jar tomato sauce
1 cup mozzarella cheese, shredded
1 cup Romano/parmesan cheese blend
1/2 tsp Italian seasoning

Instructions

Preheat oven to 400 degrees. Line oven safe baking dish (9 x13 inches) with foil and set aside.

In small mixing bowl, mix breadcrumbs and water. Set aside.

Gently mix ground meat, garlic, breadcrumb mixture, eggs, cheese, salt and pepper.

Roll mixture into tablespoon size meatballs.

Spray foil-lined casserole dish (9 x13 inches) with cooking spray and place formed meatballs on foil. Bake for 20 minutes Lower temp to 375 degrees.

Place meatballs on a plate and remove foil from baking dish.

Pour ½ cup sauce in the bottom of baking dish, spread to cover.

Place meatballs in single layer, pour remaining sauce over top of meatballs.

Cover meatballs with cheeses and sprinkle Italian seasoning on top.

Cover pan with another piece of foil and bake for 20 minutes.

Remove foil and bake uncovered for another 20 minutes.

You may place pan in broiler for an extra minute or two after baking to slightly brown the cheese.

Meatball Parmesan Bake

If you want to skip frying the eggplant, this is a great alternative.

Eggplant Parmesan for Slow Cooker

Ingredients

4 eggplants, peeled & cut into ½ inch slices
1 tbsp salt (or as needed)
2 eggs
1/3 cup water
3 tbsp all-purpose flour
1/3 cup seasoned breadcrumbs
½ cup parmesan cheese, grated
1 (32 oz) jar prepared marinara sauce
1 (16 oz package) mozzarella cheese, sliced

Instructions

Place eggplant slices in a large bowl in layers, sprinkle each layer with salt. Let stand 30 minutes to drain. Rinse and dry on paper towels.

Heat olive oil in large skillet over medium heat.

Whisk eggs with water and flour until smooth.

Dip eggplant slices in batter and fry in the hot oil until golden brown, working in batches of 2 to 3 slices at a time.

Mix seasoned breadcrumbs with parmesan cheese in a bowl.

Place ¼ of eggplant slices into slow cooker and top with ¼ of the crumbs, ¼ of the marinara sauce and ¼ of the mozzarella cheese.

Repeat layers three times more.

Cover and cook on low until tender and flavors have blended 4 to 5 hours.

Eggplant Parmesan

Tomato & Pasta Sheet Pan Roast

Ingredients

2 (10 oz.) containers cherry tomatoes, halved
2 tbsp olive oil
2 tsp freshly ground black pepper
1 tsp kosher salt
6 garlic cloves, minced
1 lb whole grain fusilli pasta
8oz. mozzarella cheese, cut into ½ inch
½ cup fresh basil, roughly chopped

Instructions

Toss to coat, spread in an even layer. Bake 20-25 minutes or until tomatoes are soft and very fragrant.

Bring a large pot of well-salted water to a boil and cook pasta per package instructions until al dente and drain.

Add cooked pasta, mozzarella, and basil to sheet pan. Toss to combine; adjust salt and pepper. Drizzle with additional oil.

Serve with ¼ cup freshly grated Parmesan cheese. Serves 8.

This is a great recipe but will take you most of the day to cook in a crock pot. Keeps your insides warm.

Slow Cooker Meatball Gnocchi Soup

Ingredients

12 oz. mild Italian sausage
¼ cup Italian seasoned breadcrumbs
¼ cup parmesan cheese, grated (plus more for topping)
28 oz. crushed tomatoes
4 cups chicken broth
½ tsp garlic powder
½ Tbs. dried basil
1 cup carrots, diced
1 celery stalk, diced
16 oz. gnocchi
fresh basil (optional)

Instructions

Combine sausage, cheese, and breadcrumbs in a medium bowl until fully mixed.

Pour the crushed tomatoes and chicken broth into the slow cooker.

Form the meat/cheese mixture into one-inch balls and drop them into liquid.

Add spices, carrots and celery and cook on low for 8 hours. After cooking for

7 hours and 30 minutes, turn the heat up to high and add the gnocchi. Continue cooking for a half hour.

Serve with grated parmesan cheese and fresh basil.

I love making my own noodles. These shells are better tasting and easier to fill than store-bought shells. Be sure to make the filling from scratch.

Manicotti Shells

Shell Ingredients

4 cups flour
½ tsp salt
4 eggs (add one at a time)
about 6 tbsp water

Instructions

Beat all ingredients together until well blended.

Put on hot grill like pancakes.

Do not get brown, just well set.

Manicotti Fillings

Cheese Filling Ingredients

1 lb. ricotta cheese
1 lb. mozzarella
grated parmesan cheese
salt & pepper
parsley
1 large egg

Instructions

Mix and fill shells

Meat Filling Ingredients

1 lb. ground beef
4-6 slices wet bread
parsley
salt & pepper
lots of garlic powder
3 eggs

Instructions

Combine ingredients. Add more bread if too soft.

Bake for 45 minutes at 350 degrees then test.

Chicken and Peppers

Ingredients

2 links (about 4 oz.) mild Italian sausage
2 tbsp olive oil
2 boneless chicken breasts
¼ tsp pepper
¾ tsp salt, divided
2 large bell peppers. sliced
2 large white onions, sliced
1 tsp garlic, chopped
¼ tsp crushed red pepper (optional)
11/4 cup chicken broth
¼ cup balsamic vinegar (white)

Instructions

Cut sausage into bite-size pieces. Preheat large pan on med-high 1 to 2 minutes.

Place oil in pan, then add sausage; cook 2 to 3 minutes until browned.

Season chicken with pepper and ½ tsp salt. Remove sausage from pan.

Place chicken in pan; cook 2 to 3 minutes on each side or until browned. Remove from pan.

Place pepper and onion, garlic, and crushed pepper in pan. Cook 2 to 3 minutes or until onions and peppers are tender.

Return sausage and chicken to pan; stir in broth, vinegar and remaining ¼ tsp salt.

Reduce heat to low; cook 5 to 6 minutes or until mixture has reduced by one-half and chicken is done. Remove chicken from pan.

Slice chicken. Serve with broth and pepper mixture.

Chicken and Peppers

SOUPS

If you have veggies in the fridge that are on their last days....this is the perfect recipe to use them all up. Very healthy.

Beef Vegetable Soup

Ingredients

2 lbs. beef chuck w or w/o bone
6 cups water
1 or 2- 8oz cans whole tomatoes
2 medium onions, chopped
1 cup celery, sliced
2 garlic toes, minced
1 tbsp salt
½ tsp black pepper
Mixed assortment of frozen veggies - e.g.: green beans, corn, sliced carrots, lima beans, peas, etc.
Cooked pasta (your choice)

Instructions

Cut beef in 1-inch cubes.

Place beef and next 7 ingredients in Dutch oven. Simmer covered for 2 hours or until meat is tender.

In last ¾ hour, add remaining vegetables (usually frozen).

When done, add cooked pasta to bowls.

Add soup serving over pasta and serve.

Italian Sausage Soup with Tortellini

Ingredients

1lb sweet Italian sausage, casings removed
1 cup onion, chopped
2 cloves garlic, minced
5 cups beef broth
½ cup water
½ cup red wine
4 large tomatoes, peeled, seeded, and chopped
1 cup carrots, thinly sliced
½ tbsp packed fresh basil leaves
½ tsp dried oregano
1 (8oz) can tomato sauce
1 ½ cups zucchini, sliced
8oz fresh tortellini pasta
3 tbsp fresh parsley, chopped

Instructions

In a 5-quart Dutch oven, brown sausage. Remove sausage and drain, reserving 1 tbsp of the drippings.

Sauté onions and garlic in drippings.

Stir in beef broth, water, wine, tomatoes, carrots, basil, oregano, tomato sauce and sausage. Bring to a boil. Reduce heat, simmer uncovered for 30 minutes.

Skim fat from the soup.

Stir in zucchini and parsley.

Simmer covered for 30 minutes. Add tortellini during last 10 minutes.

Sprinkle with parmesan cheese on top of each serving.

One of Mama Josie's best! It made me feel much better after a hard day battling the cops.

Hamburg Soup

Ingredients

1 ½ lbs ground turkey
2 stalks celery, chopped
2 carrots, chopped
1 onion, chopped
2 cans navy beans
2 cans green beans
1 can pinto beans
1 large can diced tomatoes
2 large cans tomato sauce
1 boneless chicken

Instructions

Place ingredients in crockpot and add 4 cups water

Cook on high 3 – 4 hours.

Mushroom Stew

Ingredients

2 pounds beef, cut into stew size pieces
2 pounds Italian sausage, cut into ¼ inch pieces
32 oz. container of beef broth
1 bunch celery, chopped into small pieces
2 containers fresh mushrooms sliced
3 or 4 onions, chopped
4 or 5 green peppers, cut into pieces
Garlic, grated

Instructions

Add 2 tbs. olive oil to large saucepan and brown meat.

When browned, add 2 large cans tomato sauce and one can water. Enough to make the broth hearty.

Simmer until meat is tender then add beef broth

Cook 2 to 3 hours on medium-low until veggies are tender.

Add salt, pepper, and two tsp grated garlic. Grated cheese or shredded cheese may be added as a topping.

This recipe is not very difficult to make, and you can always kick up the zing by using hot Italian sausage instead of mild.

Noodle Soup or Stew

Ingredients

1 lb mild Italian sausage
2 large boneless chicken breasts
1 package frozen onions and peppers
2 cartons of beef broth
1 large can tomato puree
½ bag egg noodles
¼ tsp pepper
1 tbsp garlic powder
1 tbsp olive oil

Instructions

Cut sausage in 1-inch pieces

Cut chicken into bite-size pieces

Place in Dutch oven and add olive oil and all cut-up meat. Cook on medium, turning several times until all is gently browned.

Add frozen onion and peppers and simmer for 45 minutes. Add beef broth, pepper, garlic powder and tomato puree. Cook for another hour on medium, then add egg noodles.

If you prefer stew texture, cook until noodles are tender.

If you prefer soup, cook noodles in separate pan of water until tender and then add salt & pepper to your taste.

Hamburger (Poor Man's) Soup

Ingredients

2lbs. ground beef
1/2 tsp salt
1/4 tsp pepper
1/8 tsp seasoned salt
1 pkg onion soup mix
6 cups boiling water
1 8-oz can tomato sauce
4 carrots, cut up
1 cup celery, sliced
1 cup elbow macaroni

Instructions

Brown hamburger in large saucepan - drain fat. Add seasoning & onion soup mix

Stir in boiling water & tomato sauce, then cover and let simmer for approx. 15 minutes

Add the celery & carrots to the mixture.

Continue to cook for 30 minutes.

Add macaroni and simmer 30 minutes longer. Add more water as necessary and stir occasionally.

You may add other veggies if desired.

If you want something from south of the boarder and have several hours on your hands, this is the perfect recipe.

Crock Pot Chicken Tortilla Soup

Ingredients

28 oz can crushed tomatoes
3 cups chicken stock
1 pre-purchased package DIY Taco seasoning
16 oz. can kidney beans, drained
15.5 can black beans, drained
11 oz, corn (not in liquid, vacuum packed)
1 lb boneless and skinless chicken breasts

Instructions

Mix all ingredients together in a crock pot and cook on low for 5 hours.

At end of cooking time, remove the chicken from the crock pot, shred, and return to the soup.

Serve topped with light sour cream and shredded cheese.

Easy Italian Stew

Ingredients

2 tbsp zesty Italian dressing
1 lb. Italian sausage (bulk)
2 cans (141/2 oz. each) fat-free reduced-sodium chicken broth
1 pkg (16 oz.) frozen stir-fry vegetables (white onions, sliced green and yellow peppers)
1 can (15 oz.) cannellini beans, rinsed
1 can (14-1/2 oz.) Italian-style diced tomatoes, undrained
1 cup elbow macaroni, uncooked
1 cup low-moisture part-skim mozzarella cheese, shredded

Instructions

Heat dressing in large saucepan on medium heat. Add sausage; cook 8 to 10 minutes or until done, stirring occasionally to break in small pieces. Drain.

Add broth, stir-fry vegetables, beans, and tomatoes; bring to boil. Stir in macaroni.

Simmer on medium heat 8 to 10 minutes or until macaroni is tender, stirring occasionally.

Serve with cheese.

Broccoli-Cheese Soup

Ingredients

½ cup onion, chopped
2 tbsp margarine
1 lb pkg Velveeta cheese
1 10-ounce bag frozen broccoli

Instructions

Sauté onions in margarine.

Add all ingredients and put in crock pot on low for 3-4 hours.

Broccoli-Cheese Soup

Hearty Italian Sausage Soup

Ingredients

1 ½ lbs of mild Italian sausage
1 onion, chopped
2 cloves garlic, minced
2 cans (14 oz each) fat-free, reduced-sodium chicken broth
1 ½ cups water
1 can (15 oz) cannellini beans, rinsed
1 can (14.5 oz) stewed tomatoes, undrained
1 cup rotini pasta, uncooked
2 cups tightly packed, torn stemmed kale
2/3 cup mozzarella cheese, shredded

Instructions

Cook sausage and onions in large skillet on medium heat 8 minutes or until sausage is evenly browned, stirring frequently and adding the garlic for the last minute.

Add broth, water, beans, and tomatoes, mix well. Bring to a boil, stirring occasionally.

Add pasta and stir. Return to boil, simmer on medium-low heat 10 minutes or until pasta is tender, stirring occasionally. Remove from heat.

Stir in kale, cover. Let stand 5 minutes or until the kale is slightly wilted.

Serve topped with cheese.

Sausage Soup

Mama Josie would make my brother and me ham and cheese sandwiches in the summer. But in the winter, she would prepare this chowder that is absolutely delicious!

Ham and Cheese Chowder

Ingredients

1½ lb (about 3 med.) potatoes, peeled and diced
¼ tsp baking soda
3 tbsp butter
1 small onion (finely chopped)
3 tbsp all-purpose flour
3 ½ cups whole milk
1 cup Velveeta cheese, cubed
½ cup sharp cheddar cheese, shredded
1 ½ cup fully cooked ham
fresh chives, minced
ground pepper

Instructions

Place potatoes and baking soda in large saucepan. Add water to cover, bring to a boil. Reduce heat and cook uncovered until tender-6 to 8 minutes. Drain, reserving ½ cup potato water.

In same saucepan, sauté onion in butter until tender, 2 to 4 minutes. Stir in flour until blended, cook and stir 2 minutes. Gradually stir in milk to potato water. Bring to a simmer, stirring constantly.

Cook and stir until thickened, 1 to 2 minutes.

Stir in cheese until melted. Stir in ham and potatoes. Heat through. If desired, top with chives and pepper.

Traditionally, this is made from dried beans, but we are using canned beans to make it easy.

Pasta Fagioli

Ingredients

2 stalks celery, chopped
1 onion, chopped
3 cloves garlic, minced
2 tsp dried parsley
1 tsp Italian seasoning
¼ tsp crushed red pepper flakes
salt to taste
1 (14.5oz) can chicken broth
2 medium tomatoes, peeled and chopped
1 (8oz) can tomato sauce
½ cup uncooked pasta (I prefer bows)
1 (15 oz) can cannellini beans, with liquid

Instructions

In a large saucepan over medium heat, cook celery, onion, garlic, parsley, Italian seasoning, red pepper and salt until onion is translucent.

Stir in chicken broth, tomatoes, and tomato sauce and simmer on low for 15 to 20 minutes.

Add pasta and cook 10 minutes, until pasta is tender

Add undrained beans and mix well. Heat through.

Serve with grated parmesan cheese sprinkled on top.

SALADS

Macaroni Fruit Salad

Ingredients

½ cup Acini-de-pepe (macaroni)
1 large can pineapple, drained (save juice)
1 large can mandarin oranges, drained (save juice)
¾ cup sugar
2 tbsp flour
2 eggs
dash salt
8 oz. Cool Whip

Instructions

Cook macaroni until done. Rinse in cold water and drain well.

Drain pineapple and oranges. Put juice in pot with sugar, flour, eggs and dash of salt.

Cook until thick.

Pour over drained macaroni, stir, and refrigerate overnight.

Add the fruit and 8 oz. container of Cool Whip the next day.

This makes for a great side dish in the summer time. Be sure to let it stand for at least 4 hours in the refrigerator before serving. If you have the time, let it stand 12 hours to allow the flavors to really blend together.

Pasta Salad

Ingredients

1 head cauliflower, broken into small pieces
2 bunches broccoli, cut up
2 cucumbers, sliced
1 dozen grape tomatoes
2-3 celery stalks, sliced
1 lb. vegetable spiral pasta
1 pkg pepperoni, sliced
1 lb. sharp cheese, cut into pieces
1 can black pitted olives, drained
2 pkg Good Seasons Italian dressing mix.

Instructions

Wash vegetables and cut cauliflower and broccoli into bite-size pieces. The cucumber may be peeled if you prefer, then sliced.

Set aside in large salad bowl.

Wash tomatoes and celery, dry on paper towel, then slice celery into bite-size pieces.

Cut sliced pepperoni in half.

Now add all ingredients except Italian dressing into large bowl.

Boil the pasta until nearly done. Run cold water over until cooled down and add to large bowl.

Empty two Good Seasons packets to bowl, then add liquid on box Instructions for one packet.

If not wet enough, you may want to add again the same as Instructions on Good Seasons box.

Refrigerate at least 4 hours before serving.

Pasta Salad

With only 4 ingredients, this can be prepared in less than 10 minutes and then left in the refrigerator for a day before serving. This is one of my favorite salads, but then again, I love artichokes!

Artichoke Salad

Ingredients

1 can artichokes in water
1 jar marinated artichokes
1 can medium pitted olives
1 small can pimentos

Instructions

Squeeze water out of the artichokes in water can.

Add to the marinated artichokes in a bowl.

Drain and add the olives.

Add chopped pimentos to bowl.

Season with garlic, salt, onion salt, etc.

Let stand in refrigerator a day before serving.

Carrot-Raisin Salad

Ingredients

2 cups raw carrots, shredded
½ cup seedless raisins
¼ cup mayonnaise
¼ cup low-fat yogurt
2 tbsp fresh lemon juice
1/8 tsp salt

Instructions

Scrub the carrots, scrape them and shred to make 2 cups.

Combine with raisins.

Mix mayonnaise, yogurt, lemon juice and salt.

Pour over salad and mix thoroughly.

Makes 6 servings.

Don't think this takes 24 hours to make. It only takes about 10 minutes to prepare and then you refrigerate for 24 hours.

Twenty-four Hour Fruit Salad

Ingredients

1 egg
2 tbsp vinegar
2 tbsp sugar
1 cup whipping cream
10 maraschino cherries, cut in half
5 oz. small marshmallows
32 oz fruit cocktail, drained
3 apples, diced
11 oz mandarin orange slices, drained
8 oz pineapple chunks, drained
1 banana, sliced

Instructions

Mix and cook egg, vinegar, and sugar until thickened. Add whipped cream and mix well.

Add all the other ingredients and chill.

This is good if made the day before and refrigerated overnight.

Chicken Salad

Ingredients

1 lb boneless and skinless chicken breasts
1 lb boneless and skinless chicken thighs
1 cup celery, sliced
1 cup salad dressing or mayonnaise
1 tbsp lemon juice
1 tbsp mustard
4 boiled eggs, chopped

Instructions

After cooking chicken, slice, cube or prepare in food processor to desired texture.

Mix chicken, celery, salad dressing or mayonnaise, lemon juice, mustard and chopped eggs in a large bowl.

Add pepper, salt, or seasoned salt according to taste. If not moist enough, add more mayonnaise (or salad dressing) one tablespoon at a time.

Makes enough salad for 20 sandwiches.

Chicken Salad

Cole Slaw

Ingredients

1 cup sugar
1 cup vinegar
¾ cup Wesson oil
1 tsp salt
1 tsp celery seed
1 tsp mustard seed
1 medium head cabbage, shredded

Instructions

Bring sugar, vinegar, oil, salt, celery seed and mustard seed to a boil and while hot, pour over shredded cabbage.

Cool and let set in refrigerator overnight.

Coleslaw

Use late-summer eggplant for this recipe.

Eggplant Salad

Ingredients

1 large eggplant, peeled
1 stalk celery
1 small onion
1 clove garlic
2 tbsp cooking oil
1 cup tomatoes
½ cup Spanish olives

Instructions

Cut eggplant in inch cubes and braise in one tablespoon oil until tender. Set aside.

Cut celery in half-inch slices, sliver onions, chop garlic very fine, add salt and pepper to taste. Braise all together in one tablespoon of oil until tender.

Add the eggplant and tomatoes, simmer 20 minutes. Remove from fire, add olives.

Refrigerate overnight to enhance flavor.

Before serving, sprinkle with grated cheese for richer flavor.

Santa Maria Salad

Ingredients

2 cups Italian bread cubes
1 8-oz bottle Kraft Italian Dressing
2 quarts. Torn assorted greens
2 cups cauliflower, sliced
2 cups broccoli flowerets
1 ½ cups zucchini, sliced

Instructions

Toss the bread cubes with ¼ cup dressing.

Bake on cookie sheet at 350 degrees 20 minutes, turning occasionally.

Combine bread cubes and remaining ingredients with 1/3 cup dressing in salad bowl, toss lightly.

Serve with additional dressing, if desired.

Makes 4 to 6 servings

Sparkling Fruit Mold

Ingredients

1 16-oz. can peach slices
1 81/4- oz. can pineapple chunks
2 3-oz.pkgs. orange flavored gelatin
11/4 cups boiling water
¾ cup sparkling rose wine or ginger ale
1 cup miniature marshmallows
1 cup heavy cream, whipped
½ cup Miracle Whip salad dressing

Instructions

Drain fruit, reserve syrup. Dissolve gelatin in boiling water. Add wine.

Add cold water to syrup to make 1 ¾ cups; stir into gelatin.

Chill until partially set, fold in fruit.

Pour into 2-quart bowl. Chill until firm.

Fold marshmallows and whipped cream into salad dressing.

Spoon over gelatin; chill.

Garnish with toasted shredded coconut, if desired.

Watermelon Salad with Feta

Ingredients

3 cups watermelon
1 1/2 cups cucumber, sliced and seeds removed
2 tbsp mint, thinly sliced or small mint leaves
1/3 cup feta cheese, crumble
3 tbsp olive oil
1 tbsp lime juice
salt and pepper to taste

Instructions

Place the watermelon, cucumber, and mint in a large bowl.

In a small bowl, whisk together the olive oil, lime juice and salt and pepper.

Drizzle the dressing over the melon mixture and toss to coat.

Sprinkle with the feta and serve.

Melon Salad

This is a very simple fruit salad that your guests will be raving about long after your party.

Mandarin Salad

Ingredients

2 1-lb containers cottage cheese
1 16 oz container Cool Whip
2 3oz. packages orange Jello
2 15 oz. cans mandarin oranges, drained
1 cup walnuts, chopped

Instructions

In large bowl, mix cottage cheese and Cool Whip together until well combined.

Add rest of ingredients until completely mixed, making sure Jello granules are dissolved.

Refrigerate until ready to eat.

BREADS & DESSERTS

This is delicious and easy to make. Be sure to use fresh, tart apples.

Auntie's German Apple Cake

Ingredients

1 boxed yellow cake mix (reserved small amount of dry mix)
2 eggs
oil for cake
4 or 5 tart apples, peeled & sliced
sugar
cinnamon
dab of butter (optional)

Instructions

Mix cake mix according to instructions. Grease bottom of 9 X 13-inch baking pan.

Sprinkle with small amount dry cake mix. Pour half cake batter, then place ½ apple slices, sprinkle apples with sugar and cinnamon.

Now pour rest of cake batter, sprinkle with dry cake mix, then place rest of apples.

Sprinkle with sugar & cinnamon.

Dot top with 2-3 dabs butter.

Bake at 350 degrees until inserted knife removes clean.

Serve warm & top with whipped cream or vanilla ice cream.

German Apple Cake

This is one of my comfort foods, especially around the holidays. It's almost better than homemade eggnog. You can also sprinkle a little nutmeg or cinnamon on top for a finishing touch.

Baked Custard

Ingredients

3 eggs, slightly beaten
¼ cup sugar
2 cups milk, scalded
½ tsp vanilla

Instructions

Combine eggs, sugar and ¼ tsp salt. Slowly stir in lightly cooled milk and vanilla.

Fill six 5-ounce custard cups; set in shallow pan on oven rack.

Pour hot water into pan 1 inch deep.

Bake at 325 degrees for 40 – 45 minutes, or till knife inserted off center comes out clean.

Serve warm or chilled.

To unmold chilled custard, loosen edge; then slip point of knife downside to let air in. Invert.

For one large custard, bake in 1-quart casserole for 1 hour.

My family members tell me there is no better banana pudding recipe than this one.

Banana Pudding

Ingredients

1 package vanilla pudding mix
6 ripe bananas
1 large box vanilla wafers
1 container whipped topping

Instructions

Cook vanilla pudding according to package instructions. Let cool.

Line a baking dish with vanilla wafers.

Slice two bananas and place over wafers

Add half whipped topping to cooled pudding mixture. Put half of pudding mixture over bananas.

Repeat layers of wafers, bananas, and rest of pudding mixture.

Arrange the last two sliced bananas on top. Add rest of whipped topping.

Refrigerate until serving.

Another Mama Josie favorite. If you want to add a little more zip to this recipe, try throwing in a handful of golden raisins.

Bread Pudding with Whiskey Sauce

Ingredients

4 cups milk
1 cup sugar
1 tsp cinnamon
3 eggs
2 tbsp butter, melted
1 loaf stale Italian bread, sliced thick
Whiskey Sauce
1 cup sugar
1 cup heavy cream
dash cinnamon
1 tbsp butter
½ tsp cornstarch
¼ cup water
1 tbsp bourbon whiskey

Instructions

Prepare pudding by combining milk, sugar, cinnamon, and eggs. Stir in melted butter. Pour mixture over bread slices and soak until all pieces are soft.

Butter a baking pan. Sprinkle a little sugar in bottom of pan before adding soaked bread.

Layer bread in pan. Bake at 325 degrees for about 45 minutes or until set.

While pudding is baking, make whiskey sauce. Combine cornstarch and water. Add to sugar mixture. Cook, stirring constantly, until sauce is clear and slightly thickened.

Remove from heat and stir in whiskey. Pour over pudding when warm.

Cranberry Freeze

Ingredients

3 ½ cup cranberries, ground or finely chopped
1 ¾ cup sugar
8 oz. can crushed pineapple, undrained
8 oz. package cream cheese, softened
1 cup whipped cream
½ cup walnuts, chopped

Instructions

In a large bowl, combine cranberries and sugar. Stir in pineapple and walnuts.

In a separate bowl, blend cream cheese, gradually add cranberry mixture. Mix until well blended.

Spread into 9 x13-inch pan and freeze. Cut into squares before serving.

When I was growing up, I had a friend from the neighborhood whose grandmother used to make these on a regular basis.

Kolacky

Ingredients

1 stick oleo, softened
1 cup flour
1 3oz cream cheese
1 can solo fruit for filling

Instructions

Mix cream cheese and oleo until smooth. Mix in flour and blend well.

Divide into two balls and chill for 1 hour.

Roll out dough. Cut into 21/2-inch squares.

Place small amount of filling in middle. Bring opposite corners together.

Press to seal.

Bake at 350 degrees 16 to 18 minutes on ungreased cookie sheet until light brown.

Cool then sprinkle with confectionary sugar or frosting.

These little guys are terrific for a party or a wedding. You can replace the vanilla with almond extract or anise if you prefer.

Italian Cookies

Ingredients

½ cup butter, softened
½ cup white sugar
3 eggs
2 tsp vanilla extract
3 cups all-purpose flour

Instructions

Preheat oven to 350 degrees. Grease cookie sheets.

In a large bowl, cream together butter and sugar until smooth. Mix in the egg and vanilla.

Combine the flour and baking powder; stir into the creamed mixture until blended.

Divide dough into walnut-sized portions.

Roll each piece into a rope and then shape into a loop.

Place cookies 2 inches apart on prepared cookie sheets.

Bake 8 to 10 minutes in preheated oven until firm and golden brown at the edges.

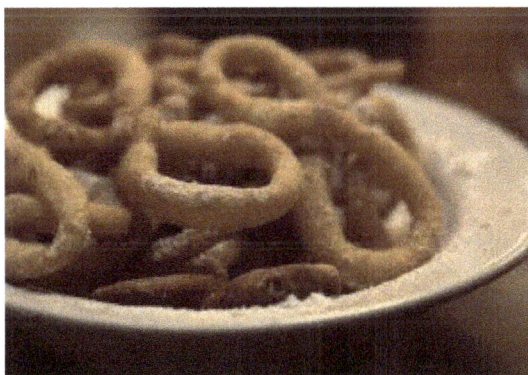

Italian Cookies

Cannoli & Filling

Ingredients

2 cups flour
Pinch of salt
pinch of baking powder
3 tbsp sugar
1 shot glass whiskey
½ tsp vinegar
1 tsp vanilla
1 orange rind, grated

Instructions

Mix flour, salt, and baking powder. Add eggs and remainder of ingredients.

Put strips around stick 3 inches longs and 1 inch in diameter. Fry in fat until brown.

Remove from sticks and cool.

Cannoli Filling

Ingredients

2 lbs. fine ricotta
½ box conf. sugar
½ package chocolate chips
½ tsp vanilla

Instructions

Beat with eggbeater till creamy.

Powdered sugar may be sifted on filled shells.

Garnish with cherry halves, chopped nuts, etc.

Connolis with filling

When making this, I like to add pumpkin mix with cinnamon and nutmeg. Your choice.

Three-step Philly Cheesecake

Ingredients

2 8 oz. packages cream cheese, softened
½ cup sugar
½ tsp vanilla
2 eggs
1 pre-purchased 9-inch graham cracker crust

Instructions

Mix cream cheese, sugar, and vanilla at medium speed with electric mixer until well blended. Add eggs and mix well.

Pour into crust.

Bake at 350 degrees for 40 minutes or until center is almost set.

Cool, refrigerate 3 hours or overnight.

Flavor Variations

Pumpkin-mix – ½ cup canned pumpkin, ½ tsp ground cinnamon and dash each ground cloves and nutmeg in with cream cheese.

Chocolate Cherry – Stir 4 squares semi-sweet chocolate, melted into batter. Top baked cheesecake with 1 can (21oz) cherry pie filling.

Chocolate Chip – Stir ½ cup mini semi-sweet chocolate chips into batter. Sprinkle with ¼ cup chips before baking.

Cheesecake

Chocolate Chip Cheesecake

This pie crust is fabulous. Flakey golden brown with terrific flavor. You can use this to make your favorite pie, whether it's apple, pumpkin, or cherry.

Wesson Oil Pie Crust

Ingredients

2 cups flour
½ cup Wesson oil
¼ cup milk
9-inch pie tin

Instructions

Combine oil and milk in 1-cup container. Add 2 cups flour. Mix with a fork then with hands (do not knead).

Divide in half.

Add more flour if dough feels real sticky.

Roll between 2 pieces waxed paper. If dough sticks to paper, put a knife between dough and paper. It should slide right off.

Fold in half and place over pie plate.

Prick bottom of crust with fork.

Bake at 375 degrees for 10 – 15 minutes until golden brown

Boston Cream Poke Cake

Ingredients

1 box yellow cake mix (along with box ingredients)
2 - ¾ oz boxes of instant vanilla pudding mix
4 cups milk
1 container chocolate frosting

Instructions

Prepare cake in 9 x13-inch pan according to box instructions.

Use spoon handle to poke holes evenly across cake.

Combine milk and pudding mix and whisk until well blended.

Pour pudding over cake, making sure it gets down into holes.

Refrigerate cake for several hours to allow pudding to settle and set up.

Open frosting container and remove foil seal. Microwave for 15 seconds and stir. Repeat until frosting is pourable.

Pour over pudding layer and spread with spatula to cover completely.

Refrigerate for at least several more hours.

Sweet Potato Casserole

An absolute must on Thanksgiving.

Sweet Potato Casserole

Casserole Ingredients

3 cups canned sweet potatoes, boiled and mashed
2 eggs, well beaten
1 cup white sugar
½ cup evaporated milk
½ tsp vanilla
½ tsp cinnamon

Topping Ingredients

1 cup brown sugar
½ cup flour
½ stick margarine
1 cup nuts, chopped

Instructions

Combine first 7 ingredients and mix well.

Pour into 9 x 9-inch pan.

Mix topping well and put over top of first mixture

Bake at 400 degrees for 30 minutes.

Apple Walnut Cake

Ingredients

4 cups apples, coarsely chopped
2 cups sugar
2 eggs
½ cup Mazola oil
2 tsp vanilla
2 cups sifted flour
2 tsp baking powder
2 tsp cinnamon
1 tsp salt
1 cup walnuts, chopped

Instructions

Combine apples and sugar and let stand.

Beat eggs slightly.

Add oil and vanilla.

Mix salt, baking powder, cinnamon and flour that is sifted. Stir in apples and sugar mixture.

Add walnuts.

Pour into greased and floured 14 x 9-inch pan or waxed paper lined.

Bake at 350 degrees 45-50 minutes or until done.

Let stand in pan until cool.

Frost with pre-purchased whipped cream or vanilla frosting.

Apple Walnut Cake

One time a guy called me a cream puff. He wasn't able to talk again for a while afterward. This recipe is a knockout.

Cream Puffs

Ingredients

½ cup butter or margarine
1 cup boiling water
1 cup sifted all-purpose flour
¼ tsp salt
4 eggs

Instructions

Melt butter in 1 cup boiling water.

Add flour and salt all at once; stir vigorously.

Cook and stir till mixture forms a ball that doesn't separate.

Remove from heat; cool slightly.

Add eggs, one at a time, beating after each till smooth.

Drop heaping tablespoons 3 inches apart on greased cookie sheet.

Bake at 400 degrees until golden brown and puffy, about 30 minutes.

Remove from oven, split.

Cool on rack.

When completely cooled, fill with favorite pudding.

Makes 10 puffs

Cream Puffs

These go great with Hamburger Soup or Poor Man's Stew (See Soups section).

Fluffy Dumplings

Ingredients

1 cup sifted all-purpose flour
2 tsp baking powder
½ tsp salt
½ cup milk
2 tbsp salad oil

Instructions

Sift flour, baking powder and salt together into a mixing bowl.

Combine milk and salad oil; add all at once to dry ingredients, stirring just till moistened.

Drop from tbsp atop bubbling stew. Cover tightly.

Let mixture return to boiling (don't lift cover).

Simmer 12-15 minutes.

Makes 10 dumplings

Potato Dumplings

Ingredients

4 potatoes
salt & pepper
¼ cup onion, grated
2 tsp parsley
6 large eggs

Instructions

Boil potatoes in water 2 minutes.

Set aside 10 minutes to cool then grate by hand.

In large bowl, combine egg whites, onion, parsley, salt, and pepper.

Spray large skillet with cooking spray.

Cook 1/3 cup mixture in pan, cook until golden brown-4 minutes each side.

Potato Dumplings

Fruit Dump Cake

Ingredients

1 box yellow cake mix
4 cups fresh fruit (strawberries, blueberries, raspberries, blackberries, your choice)
½ cup sugar
½ cup butter, melted
1 tsp ground cinnamon

Instructions

Pre-heat oven to 350 degrees.

Mix berries, sugar and cinnamon in bottom 9 x 13-inch pan.

Cover berries with dry cake mix. Pour butter over cake mix.

DO NOT STIR

Bake for 30 minutes or until light brown.

Serve warm or cold.

Top with Cool Whip or ice cream.

This can be addictive, so watch out.

Ice Cream Bread

Ingredients

1 pint maple walnut ice cream
1.5 cups self-rising flour

Instructions

Stir ice cream and flour together. Spoon into a buttered, floured pan (8 x 4 inches).

Bake at 350 degrees for 40 minutes.

Remove bread from pan and cool thoroughly.

Makes one loaf.

You can buy fluted tins to bake these in or use a standard muffin tin. Don't even think about only eating one!

Pusties

Ingredients

2 ¼ cup Spry or Crisco
2 cups brown sugar
½ cup white sugar
¼ cup honey
2 eggs
½ cup water
7 ½ cups flour
1 ½ tsp baking powder

Mix Spry (Crisco), brown sugar, white sugar, and honey well and add 2 eggs, ½ cup water.

Mix and add 7 ½ cups flour and 1½ tsp baking powder. Mix well and form crust in each bottom pusti tin.

Filling Ingredients

1½ cups flour
2¼ cups sugar
1 cup cocoa

Instructions

Mix well and add 6 cups milk. Cook until thick. Put 2 egg yolks in a cup and add 3 tsp vanilla. Mix into pudding.

Cool.

Fill pusti ¾ full. Form top crust and seal to bottom crust.

Pierce top crust. Brush tops with egg white. Bake at 400 degrees, for 20 to 25 minutes.

You may also use pie filling.

7-up Biscuits

Ingredients

4 cups Bisquick
1 cup sour cream
1 cup 7-up soda
½ cup butter, melted

Instructions

Mix Bisquick, sour cream and 7-up. Dough will be soft – don't fret.

Knead and fold dough until coated with your baking mix.

Cut biscuits using round cutter.

Pour melted butter on bottom of a cookie sheet or 9 x 13-inch pan.

Place biscuits on top of melted butter and bake for 12 -15 minutes at 425 degrees until brown.

Biscuits

OTHER KILLER RECIPES

Baked Cabbage

Ingredients

1 medium head cabbage, shredded
1 medium onion, chopped
1lb ground beef
1 cup rice (not instant)
salt & pepper to taste
1 1/2 cup boiling water
1 stick margarine
1 large or two small cans tomato sauce

Instructions

Spread half of the cabbage in greased casserole.

Fry onion in margarine.

Add rice and brown. Pour over cabbage.

Brown beef and spread over rice. Add salt and pepper.

Top with remaining cabbage and then pour tomato sauce on top.

Bake at 350 degrees for 1 hour. Can be made a day ahead.

Pour 11/2 cups boiling water over just before baking.

This has my vote for one of the best breakfasts in the world!

Biscuit & Sausage Gravy

Ingredients

1 can refrigerator biscuit (8 biscuits)
2 lbs. breakfast sausage
2 cups milk
2 tbsp flour

Instructions

Bake biscuits while sausage is frying.

Continue frying sausage until completely done.

Drain off excess fat

Add 2 tbsp flour, mix into sausage. Add milk.

Stir while milk mixes with flour and sausage. Continue until gravy is smooth and thick. Add salt and pepper to taste.

Cut biscuit in half and place on plate.

Spoon sausage gravy over biscuit and serve.

Crunchy Turkey Bake

Ingredients

2 cups croutons
2 cans cream of chicken soup
½ cup mayonnaise
1 ½ cups turkey (or chicken), diced
1 pkg frozen broccoli, thawed & drained
1 cup almonds, sliced
1 4 oz can mushrooms, drained

Instructions

Spread 1cup crushed croutons in 7 x 11-inch, or 9 x 9-inch baking dish sprayed with PAM.

Combine soup and mayo, spread half over crushed croutons.

Top with meat, broccoli, almonds & mushrooms.

Spread with remaining soup mixture and croutons.

Cover with foil and bake at 350 degrees 30 – 35 minutes.

Remove foil and brown for an additional 15 minutes.

Turkey Bake

Ham & Cheese Hors d'oeuveres

Ingredients

1 lb ham, sliced
8 oz cream cheese, softened
4 oz blue cheese
1 tbsp garlic powder
2 tbsp Worcestershire sauce

Instructions

In medium size bowl, mix all ingredients except ham.

Mix until well blended and spreadable.

Once cheese mixture has reached the right consistency, spread over each slice of ham.

Roll each cheese and ham slice until all are done.

Place toothpick approximately 1 inch apart on ham rolls.

Cut into separate 1-inch rolls.

Place on plate, cover tightly with plastic wrap and refrigerate until serving time.

Cheesy Chicken Casserole with Broccoli and Bacon

Ingredients

7 slices bacon
1 medium yellow onion, diced
3 cloves garlic
1 ½ cups fresh broccoli florets
1/3 cup butter
1/3 cup all-purpose flour
2 cups whole milk
1 ¼ cups half and half or heavy cream
2 ½ cups mozzarella cheese, divided
½ cup parmesan cheese, shredded
16 oz. box dried medium pasta shells, cooked according to package instructions
2 ½ cups chicken, shredded
¾ tsp kosher salt
½ tsp black pepper

Instructions

Preheat oven to 350 degrees. In a large, oven-safe skillet, cook bacon over medium heat until crisp.

Remove to a plate, reserving grease in skillet.

Remove all but 1 tbsp bacon grease.

To same skillet, add diced onion and cook 4 -5 minutes, until soft. Add garlic and cook for one minute, stirring very often. Remove to plate with the bacon.

Add broccoli to skillet and cook 2-3 minutes, until very bright green and heat through. Remove to plate.

Add butter and melt, then add flour and whisk to combine. Slowly pour in milk and half and half, whisking until all flour mixture is incorporated.

Cook, whisking very often, until mixture has thickened (about 5 – 10 minutes).

Remove from heat and stir in 1 ¾ cups mozzarella cheese and ½ cup parmesan until melted.

Add in cooked pasta, shredded chicken, bacon, onion, broccoli, salt & pepper. Stir until combined. Top with remaining ¾ cup mozzarella cheese.

Bake 15 minutes, then broil on high for 1-2 minutes to brown cheese (optional).

Chili Con Queso Casserole

Ingredients

2 cans (4 oz each) mild whole green chilis, drained
2 cups (2 to 3 medium) tomatoes, chopped
2 cups (8 oz) cheddar cheese, shredded
1 cup Bisquick baking mix
½ cup dairy sour cream
½ cup milk
3 eggs

Instructions

Grease square baking dish, 8x8x2 inches. Remove seeds from chilies.

Arrange chilies in single layer in dish. Sprinkle with tomatoes and cheese.

Beat remaining ingredients with wire whisk or hand beater until smooth.

Pour over top. Cover and refrigerate up to 24 hours.

Heat oven to 375 degrees. Bake uncovered until knife inserted comes out clean, 35 to 40 minutes.

Makes 6 to 8 servings.

Spicy Mac and Cheese with Chicken

Ingredients

2 packages (7 ¼ oz each) Kraft Macaroni & Cheese Dinner

2 tbsp Kraft Zesty Italian Dressing

1 ½ lb boneless, skinless chicken breasts, cut into thin strips

1 white onion, cut lengthwise in half, then crosswise into thin slices, divided

1 can (14.5 oz.) diced tomatoes, undrained

1 jalapeno pepper, stemmed

1 cup sharp cheddar cheese, shredded

2 tbsp fresh cilantro, chopped

Instructions

Prepare dinners in a large saucepan as directed on package. Meanwhile, heat dressing in a large skillet on medium heat.

Add chicken and half the onions. Cook 5 -8 minutes until chicken is done, stirring frequently.

Heat oven to 350 degrees. Spoon dinners into 13 x 9-inch baking dish sprayed with cooking spray. Top with chicken mixture.

Blend tomatoes and jalapeno pepper in blender until smooth, spread over chicken mixture. Top with cheddar and cover.

Bake 30 minutes or until casserole is heated through, uncovering after 25 minutes.

Top with cilantro and remaining onions.

Mac & Cheese

Ingredients

1/4 cup butter or margarine, divided
1/4 cup flour
1 cup milk
1/2-lb (8oz) Velveeta cheese, cut into 1/2-inch cubes
2 cups elbow macaroni, cooked
1/2 cup sharp cheddar cheese, shredded
6 Ritz crackers, crushed or 1/4 cup panko breadcrumbs

Instructions

Pre-heat oven to 350 degrees.

Melt 3 tbsp butter in medium saucepan on med. heat. Whisk in flour; cook 2 minutes, stir constantly. Gradually stir in milk. Bring to boil, cook, and stir 3 to 5 minutes or until thickened. Add Velveeta; cook 3 minutes, or until melted, stirring frequently.

Stir in macaroni.

Spoon into 2 qt. casserole, sprayed with cooking spray; sprinkle with cheddar. Melt remaining butter, toss with crumbs. Sprinkle over casserole.

Bake 20 minutes or until done.

Mac and Cheese with crumbs on top

Cheesy Chicken Casserole

Ingredients

3 cups shell noodles, uncooked
3 tbsp butter
1/3 cup red bell pepper, diced
1 onion, finely diced
½ tsp seasoning salt
1 tsp seasoning salt
1 tsp chili powder
10 ¾ oz can cream of chicken soup
1 1/3 cups milk
3 cups sharp cheddar cheese, shredded and divided
1/3 cup parmesan cheese, shredded
4 oz. mild green chilis
3 cups cooked chicken

Instructions

Cook shells al dente according to package instructions

Cook onion and red pepper in butter until tender, about 5 minutes. Stir in salt and chili powder.

In a large bowl, combine soup, onion mixture, milk and 2 cups cheddar cheese and parmesan cheese. Mix well.

Stir in chicken, pasta, and green chilies.

Spread into 9 x13-inch casserole dish. Top with remaining cheese.

Bake 30 – 35 minutes or until hot and bubbly.

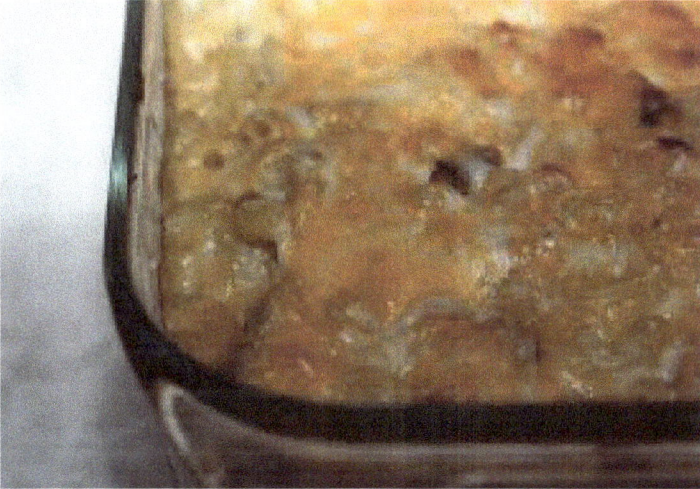

Cheesy Chicken Casserole

Krispy Coconut Chicken

Ingredients

Oil for frying (I use vegetable)
1/2 cup cornstarch
1/4 teaspoon salt
1/8 teaspoon pepper
1 tsp cayenne pepper (optional)
3 large eggs, lightly beaten
3 - 4 cups of sweetened coconut flakes (Baker's Coconut)
3 - 4 medium boneless, skinless, chicken breasts, cut into strips or nuggets.

Instructions

In a medium pot, add 2 - 3 inches of oil. Turn burner to medium high and allow oil to get nice and hot.

In a bowl mix cornstarch, salt, pepper & cayenne pepper. Set aside.

In a second bowl, add 3 eggs and lightly beat.

In a third bowl add coconut flakes.

Take chicken and douse in cornstarch mixture. Then dip into eggs and cover well. Then dip in coconut and set aside on a plate. Do this to all chicken.

Once chicken is ready, check oil. Place the end of a wooden spoon in the oil. If bubbles form around the spoon the oil is ready. If bubbles do not form around the spoon, then the oil is not hot enough.

Once oil is hot enough, GENTLY add chicken one piece at a time to oil, ensuring chicken does not touch and stick together upon initial contact into oil.

Cook chicken for approximately 4 minutes then flip and allow the other side to cook. Cook second side for an additional approximate 4 minutes.

Gently remove golden chicken and set on a paper towel lined plate. Cook chicken in batches if all does not fit into pan.

Once all chicken is cooked, serve with your favorite sauce.

Enjoy this plain, with honey or with orange or sweet & sour sauce.

Coconut Chicken

Pork Chops

Ingredients

4-thick pork chops
virgin olive oil
1 red bell pepper, sliced round
1 onion, sliced round
1 tsp basil
1 tsp garlic powder
1 tsp onion powder
2 tbsp red wine
¼ tsp black pepper
¼ tsp salt
1 large tomato, sliced round
½ cup flour
1 tsp soy sauce
small (14 oz) can chicken broth
2 cups rice

Instructions

Dip the pork chops in flour & brown on both sides in hot oil in deep skillet. Layer onion, red bell pepper slices over the chops.

Add basil, onion powder, garlic powder, salt, pepper, and red wine.

Add the sliced tomatoes

Cover and cook for 5 minutes.

Then add ½ cup chicken broth. Reduce heat and simmer on low for 1 hour.

Take chops out and thicken the gravy with 2 tbsp of flour and add more chicken broth. Stir in 1 tsp soy sauce. Place pork chops back in pan, cover for 2 minutes over hot steamed rice.

Serves 6

Suggested red wine: Bracco, Chianti Classico Reserva

Pork Chops

Chicken Casserole

Ingredients

3 cups cooked chicken breast, cut up
1 can cream of chicken or any creamed soup
2 to 3 cups cooked rice
½ cup carrots, chopped
¾ cup diced celery
½ cup mayonnaise
¾ to 1 cup seasoned panko
2 tbsp butter, melted

Instructions

Preheat oven to 350 degrees.

Combine all ingredients into greased 9 x13-inch baking dish.

Sprinkle breadcrumbs over top of casserole.

Drizzle melted butter over top.

Bake 30 to 40 minutes until casserole is heated through.

Who doesn't like a stuffed pepper? I have been making them since I was a kid. Mama Josie used to have me help her cut and clean the peppers while she prepared the stuffing. Delicious!

Stuffed Peppers

Ingredients

Mixture #1
4 red bell peppers
1 lb. ground beef
½ cup Romano Serve cheese
2 tbsp onion, minced
¼ cup breadcrumbs
2 cloves garlic, minced
1/8 tsp salt
½ tsp oregano
1/4 tsp pepper
1 tbsp
½ tsp basil

Mixture #2
1 ½ cup crushed tomatoes
2 tbsp olive oil
1/8 tsp Basil
½ tsp salt
1/8 tsp oregano
¼ tsp pepper
½ tsp garlic powder

Instructions

Rinse and cut peppers in half remove stems and seeds. Rinse and set aside.

Mix all of mixture #1 together well.

Fill peppers with mixture #1.

Place peppers in a 2-quart baking dish.

Next combine mixture #2 and pour around and on top of peppers

My family prefers the chicken over the traditional corn beef.

Chicken Ruben Sandwich

Ingredients

8 slices rye bread
2 boneless chicken breasts
4 oz. swiss cheese, sliced
1 lb jar sauerkraut, drained and squeezed dry
Thousand Island dressing

Instructions

Turn broiler on with rack 4 inches from heat.

Top 4 slices bread with cheese, chicken, and sauerkraut. Spoon dressing over sauerkraut. Place remaining bread on top.

Broil sandwiches about 2 minutes each side until cheese has melted and is golden brown.

Cut in half and serve immediately.

Mama Josie made these several times a year. Sometimes she would throw in some mushrooms and a touch of white wine. Something to think about.

Easy Creamed Onions

Ingredients

¾ cup water
salt to taste
2 cups onions (fresh preferred), peeled
¼ cup butter
1 ½ cup cold milk
¼ cup quick-mixing flour (such as Wondra) or more as needed

Instructions

Bring water and salt to boil in small saucepan, cook onions in the boiling water until just tender, 5 to 10 minutes. Drain, reserving ½ cup water in saucepan and return onions to pan.

Add butter to onions.

Mix milk and quick-mixing flour together in a bowl, add to onion mixture.

Cook and stir over medium-low heat until thickened, 10 to 15 minutes.

Stir in more quick-mixing flour if mixture is too thin.

This only takes about 30 minutes and is a super satisfying skillet supper. Some say pierogis came from China, and others say it came from Kiev to Poland. Either way, this is one delicious supper.

Pierogi Chicken Supper

Ingredients

1 pkg (16 oz) frozen pierogis
1 lb. boneless chicken breast, cut into 2 x ½- inch strips
1/8 tsp pepper
2 tbsp butter, divided
1 large, sweet onion, thinly sliced
½ cup cheddar cheese, shredded

Instructions

Cook pierogi according to box instructions (drain well)

Toss chicken with pepper in large skillet, heat 1 tbsp butter over medium heat; sauté' chicken and onions until chicken is no longer pink and remove.

In same saucepan, heat rest of butter over medium heat. Saute'pierogis until light brown. Stir in chicken mix. Sprinkle with cheese and cover. Remove from heat and let stand until cheese melts.

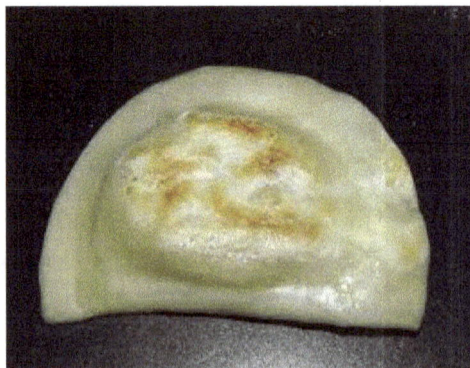

Perogi

Fried Irish Cabbage with Bacon

Ingredients

1(12oz.) package bacon
¼ cup bacon drippings
1 small head cabbage, cored & finely chopped
ground pepper to taste

Instructions

Cook bacon in a deep skillet over medium heat until crisp, 5 to 7 minutes.

Remove bacon from skillet and drain on a paper towel-line plate. Reserve ¼ cup drippings in skillet.

Cook and stir cabbage in hot bacon drippings over medium heat until cabbage wilts,

5 -7 minutes.

Crumble bacon over cabbage. Stir and simmer until bacon is warmed, 2 to 3 minutes.

Season with black pepper.

For More News About Frank Cullotta,
Signup For Our Newsletter:

http://wbp.bz/newsletter

Word-of-mouth is critical to an author's long-
term success. If you appreciated this book please
leave a review on the Amazon sales page:

http://wbp.bz/cullottaskitchena

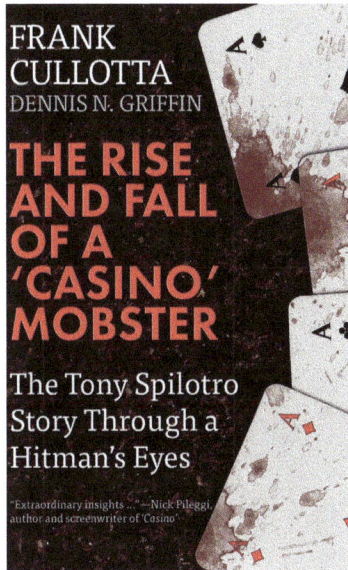

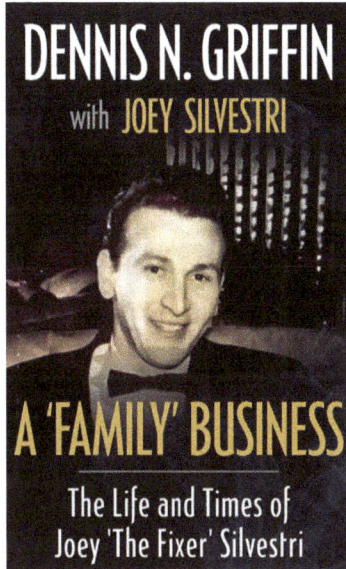

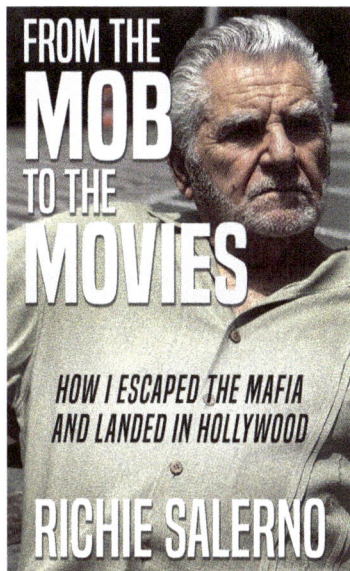

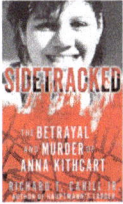

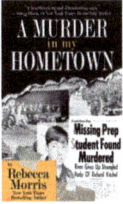

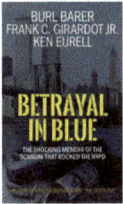